POSTCARDS · FROM ·

P9-CBA-153

Italy DISCARDED

Helen Arnold

RSVP
RAINTREE
STECK-VAUGHN
PUBLISHERS
The Steck-Vaughn Company

Austin, Texas

Published by Raintree Steck-Vaughn Publishers, an imprint of Steck-Vaughn Company

A ZOË BOOK

Editor: Kath Davies, Pam Wells
Design: Sterling Associates
Map: Julian Baker
Production: Grahame Griffiths

Library of Congress Cataloging-in-Publication Data

Arnold, Helen.
    Italy / Helen Arnold.
        p. cm. — (Postcards from)
    Includes index.
    ISBN 0-8172-4018-7 (hardcover). — ISBN 0-8172-6201-6 (softcover)
    1. Italy—Description and travel—Juvenile literature.
    1. Italy—Description and travel—Juvenile Literature. I. Title. II. Series.
DG430.2. A76 1997
914.504'929—dc20

                                             95–53974
                                                   CIP
                                                       AC

Printed and bound in the United States
1 2 3 4 5 6 7 8 9 0 WZ 99 98 97 96

Photographic acknowledgments

The publishers wish to acknowledge, with thanks, the following photographic sources:

Lesley & Roy Adkins Picture Library - cover bl, 16; Jonathan Blair / Black Star / Colorific 18; Duncan Maxwell / Robert Harding Picture Library 8; The Hutchison Library / John Egan 22; Impact Photos / Mark Cator - cover tl; / Mike McQueen - title page, 20; / Fabrizio Belluschi 10; / Roger Perry 12; / Jeremy Horner 26; Sporting Pictures 24; Zefa - cover r, 6, 14, 28.

The publishers have made every effort to trace the copyright holders, but if they have inadvertently overlooked any, they will be pleased to make the necessary arrangement at the first opportunity.

Contents

All the words that appear in **bold** are explained in the Glossary on page 30.

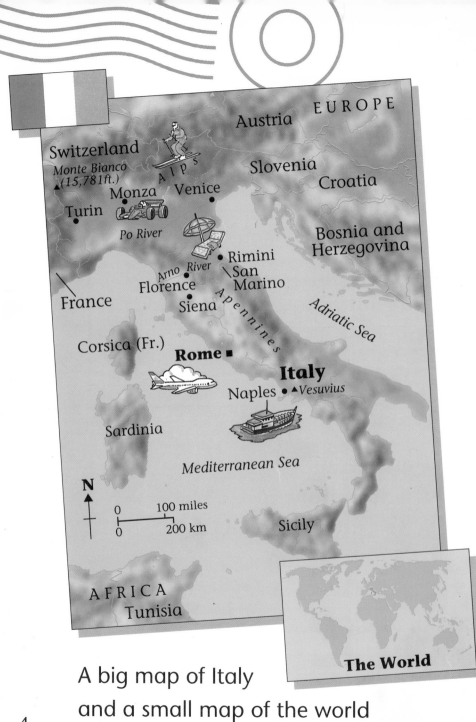

Switzerland
Monte Bianco
▲ (15,781ft.)
Turin
Monza
Venice
Po River
Austria
EUROPE
Slovenia
Croatia
Bosnia and
Herzegovina
Arno River
Florence
France
Siena
Corsica (Fr.)
Rimini
San
Marino
Apennines
Adriatic Sea
Rome ■
Italy
Naples ● ▲Vesuvius
Sardinia
Mediterranean Sea
N
0   100 miles
0   200 km
Sicily
AFRICA
Tunisia

The World

A big map of Italy
and a small map of the world

4

Dear Rita,

You can see Italy in red on the small map. It is shaped like a boot. The plane took eight hours to fly here from New York. The weather in Italy is sunny during much of the year.

Your friend,

Sam

P.S. Mom says that Italy is much smaller than the United States. There are two big **islands** called Sicily and Sardinia. They are part of Italy.

A view over the city of Rome

Dear Gary,

Here we are in Rome. It is the **capital** city of Italy. We have seen lots of old buildings. Some of them are in ruins. I threw a coin into the Trevi Fountain. It will bring me luck.

Love,

Colin

P.S. Not all the buildings in Rome are old. It is also a modern city. About three million people live here. The roads are full of noisy **traffic**.

Enjoying a meal outdoors, near Turin

Dear Bridget,

Did you know that *pizza* comes from Italy? It means "pie" in Italian. My favorite foods are spaghetti or pasta with tomato sauce and ice cream. These all come from Italy.

Your friend,

Helga

P.S. Mom loves fresh fruits and vegetables. She goes to the outdoor market to buy them. She pays for her things with Italian money called *lira*.

A policeman in the Vatican

Dear Keith,

Today we went to the Vatican. It is like a small town in the middle of Rome. The Pope lives in the Vatican. He is the head of the **Roman Catholic** Church. Many Italian people are Catholics.

Love,

Melanie

P.S. Mom says that the Vatican is ruled by the Pope. It is not part of Italy. That is why the policemen wear different uniforms.

An Italian sports car

Dear Danny,

We have been on some Italian highways. They are called *autostrada*. We had to pay a **toll** when we got off the highway. Italian people love cars. They drive very fast.

Love,

Fran

P.S. Dad says that Italy is famous for making fast cars. People make cars in the north of Italy. There are many **factories** there.

The harbor at Naples

Dear Elaine,

We are staying in Naples. It is on the west coast of Italy, right on the Mediterranean Sea. We saw fishing boats in the **harbor**. We went on a boat ride along the coast.

Love,

Nina

P.S. Mom says that Naples is a big city. In the harbor people load ships with fresh food and other goods. The ships carry these goods to be sold in countries around the world.

A street in Pompeii

Dear Hamid,

Today we went to Pompeii. It is near a **volcano** called Vesuvius. About 2,000 years ago, the volcano **erupted**. It buried the town in hot ash. We walked around the ruined town.

Yours,

Mike

P.S. Dad said we could pretend we lived in Pompeii. Everything was still in its place. You could even see cooking pots and toys.

A crowded beach near Rimini

Dear Terry,

We are on the east coast of Italy now. I have been swimming in the Adriatic Sea. Jimmy played games on the beach. Mom and Dad have been sleeping on beach chairs all day.

Love,

Amy

P.S. The shops are full of **tourists**. I bought a leather belt in a crafts shop. I could not afford a gold necklace, but there were some pretty ones.

Gondolas in Venice

Dear Brenda,

Venice is made up of hundreds of little islands. We travel around by boat. There are no cars inside the city. Some people use boats that are called *gondolas*.

Love,

Jan

P.S. Mom says we can come back to Venice in September to see the sailing races. People decorate their boats then. It is very hot here now, but it gets cold in the winter.

A statue by Michelangelo

Dear Carol,

We are staying in Florence. The old buildings are full of paintings and statues. People come from around the world to see them. The Arno River runs through the middle of Florence.

Love,

Naomi

P.S. Mom says that artists love Florence. Michelangelo and Leonardo da Vinci were famous artists. They painted pictures and made statues in Florence about 500 years ago.

A soccer match between two famous Italian teams

Dear Bruno,

Italian people love sports. They swim and sail in the summer. In the winter, they go skiing. I think they like soccer best. They have world famous soccer teams.

Your friend,

Barry

P.S. Dad loves the car races at the Monza track. There are road races, too. One race is 1,000 miles long. That is 1,600 kilometers!

The *palio* in Siena

Dear Sandra,

We went to a special horse race in Siena. It is called the *palio*. The race is held right in the middle of the old town. Thousands of people came to watch the *palio*. It was very exciting.

Love,

Lisa

P.S. Aunt Meg says that there are lots of **festivals** in Italy. Many of them have to do with religious events.

The Italian flag

Dear Lenny,

Here is the flag of Italy. It is green, white, and red. Italy does not have a king or a queen. The head of the country is called the president. This means Italy is a **republic**.

Yours,

Pietro

P.S. Mom says that the people of Italy choose their own leaders. A country ruled this way is called a **democracy**. The Italian leaders meet in Rome.

Glossary

Capital: The town or city where people who rule the country meet

Democracy: A country where all the people choose the leaders they want to run the country

Erupt: To send out hot, melted rock, smoke, and ash, from inside the Earth

Factory: A building where things are made

Festival: A time when people remember something special that happened in the past

Harbor: A place where ships dock for safety

Island: A piece of land that has water all around it

P.S.: This stands for Post Script. A postscript is the part of a card or letter that is added at the end, after the person has signed it.

Republic: A country where the people choose their leaders. A republic does not have a king or a queen.

Roman Catholic: One of many Christian faiths. The Christian people follow the teachings of Jesus. Jesus lived about 2,000 years ago.

Toll: The money you have to pay to use a road or bridge

Tourists: People who are on vacation away from home

Traffic: The cars, trucks, and bikes that carry people and goods on the road

Volcano: A mountain that is made of melted rock from inside the Earth. When a volcano erupts, the hot, melted rock comes out of a large hole, or crater, on the mountain.

Index